Refreshing Bible Study

Ideas for individuals and groups

edited by Ian Paul

Director of Partnership Development,
St John's College, Nottingham

Managing Editor, Grove Books Ltd

GROVE BOOKS LIMITED
RIDLEY HALL RD CAMBRIDGE CB3 9HU

Contents

Dr Doug Ingram is Lecturer in Old Testament at St John's College, Nottingham
Revd Dr Philip Jenson is Lecturer in Old Testament at Trinity College, Bristol
Margaret Killingray lectures at the London Institute for Contemporary Christianity
Revd Dr Jo Bailey Wells is Lecturer in Old Testament at Ridley Hall, Cambridge
Dr Mark Bonnington is Lecturer in New Testament at Cranmer Hall, Durham
Revd Dr Michael B Thompson is Vice-Principal of Ridley Hall, Cambridge

My thanks to the members of the Grove Biblical series editorial group for their lively and engaging contributions both to this booklet and to our regular discussions about the series and titles. Dedicated to Rebecca Katharine (3) whose boundless delight in life is so refreshing.
Ian Paul, March 2004

The Cover Illustration is by Peter Ashton

First Impression March 2004
ISSN 1365-490X
ISBN 1 85174 557 2

Ian Paul

Introduction

1

The worst thing that Christians can do with the Bible is to make it boring!

Here we have a work that is greater in scope than *The Lord of the Rings*, that has more adventure than *Master and Commander*, more romance than *Love Actually* and in terms of popularity and sales leaves the whole *Harry Potter* series in the shade. How can it ever become boring?!

And yet that, sadly, is often the experience of Christians. Sometimes this can arise from over-familiarity with the text, or perhaps from readers having been taught that, because this is a special, 'holy' book, it cannot be read in the ways that other books can be read, and has to be treated with a stifling deference. But more often it arises from unfamiliarity, from not quite knowing where to begin. This booklet has been borne out of the conviction that reading the Bible, both by individuals and in groups, should be an engaging, fascinating and life-changing experience. And so it aims to offer the reader a range of approaches and tools which can breathe new life into things that have become stale and give new ways forward where there is a sense of having reached a dead end.

Where Do I Begin?

When I first started reading the Bible for myself, I was taught to ask three questions of the passage I was looking at. Over the years, I have found that these three questions have served me very well; they are summarized in this diagram.

The first question is 'What is the text actually saying?' It is a question about *discovery* and it is an important one because it is remarkably easy, in these days of information overload, simply to miss what is there in front of us.

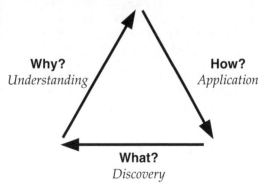

Why?
Understanding

How?
Application

What?
Discovery

The second question involves asking 'Why might it be saying this? What is the significance of this; what principle is there behind it?' This is a question (or series of questions) about *understanding*. Some of the assumptions and contexts behind different passages of the Bible are very different from ours (though it is also remarkable how much we have in common) and we need to ask this question if we are to avoid some basic mistakes in Bible reading.

The third question is 'How does this affect my life today?' and is a question of *application*. In some ways this is the most important question; without it, reading the Bible becomes nothing more than an academic exercise. But we need to learn the discipline of asking this question *after* the other two, and not short-circuit the process of reading.

Those who study the process of how we interpret the Bible sometimes talk about the world *of* the text, the world *behind* the text, and the world *in front of* the text. My three questions correspond to these three areas. Asking 'what?' involves looking at the world of the text, what it is saying, what it happening within the text itself. Asking 'why?' will often mean looking at the world behind the text to see how it would have made sense to its writers and first readers. Asking 'how?' involves engaging with the world 'in front of' the text, that is, the world of us as readers in the 21st century. The chapters that follow, in various different ways, touch on each of these three 'worlds.'

But these three questions are also related to what it means to read the Bible as a Christian. Any Christian reading must seek to make sense of what Scripture says in the light of our understanding of God as Trinity—as Father, Son and Holy Spirit.

- Since God is Father, the one who has created and established his world, what he says cannot be limited to its local and temporary significance—it must be allowed to speak across different contexts to believers in different ages.

- Since God expressed himself supremely in the life of the Son who lived at a particular time and place, our reading must take seriously the particular context of each passage of Scripture as we make sense of it.

- Since God is Spirit, alive and at work in his world today, we need to listen to what he might be saying to us through the text in our own context today, and living out the consequences.

Any reading which fails to take seriously all these aspects—of underlying principle, particular expression and contemporary application—is failing in some measure to be a properly Christian reading. The ultimate aim is that we might, together, more faithfully express the life of God in the world.

Doug Ingram

Enjoying the Story

2

It is a good thing to study the Bible in depth and detail.

But sometimes Christians get so caught up in studying individual passages (and preachers get so caught up in preaching on small and sometimes isolated texts) that the beauty and fascination—to say nothing of the power—of the Bible stories gets lost. Of course it is a good thing to try to determine what the historical context of a particular passage was. Of course it is a good thing to try to work out exactly what this or that Hebrew or Greek (or even Aramaic) word means. Of course it is a good thing to try to determine how a specific text fits into the overall 'plan of salvation.' And—of course—it is a very good thing to try to work out what relevance a biblical text you are studying has for Christian life today. (It is not my purpose here to justify all these 'of courses'!) But there is a time for simply enjoying reading the Bible, and especially responding simply as 'a reader' to the entertaining, challenging, horrific, gruesome, romantic, mysterious, deep and unfathomable stories in the Bible. (If the term 'a reader' rings warning bells, it need not, as I am not here advocating a 'reader response' approach to the Bible.)

There is a time for simply enjoying reading the Bible

The Big Story

My particular interest is the Old Testament, so that is what I will focus on. But the following comments have relevance for the New Testament, too. The first thing to note about the Old Testament is that there is a basic storyline that runs through much of it, which can be retold in a few minutes. One of the first things I do with my students is to tell the story in a variety of ways, then set them the task of retelling the basic Old Testament story in under five minutes for one of a range of audiences—primary school assembly, church housegroup, or congregation. There are a few main parts to this story, which might be headed thus:

The first thing to note about the Old Testament is that there is a basic storyline that runs through much of it

Beginnings	Early Monarchy
Early Ancestors	Divided Monarchy
Exodus and Wanderings	Collapse and Exile
Entry into the Promised Land	Return and Rebuilding
Judges Period	

Pad each of these out a bit with some more details, inserting the main characters for each phase, and you have got the 'Big Picture' in easily under five minutes. The rest of the Old Testament can then be related to this story and, indeed, it is much easier to understand when it is! It may be more complicated than this suggests, but the *basic outline* of the Old Testament story—as it is presented in the Old Testament itself—is remarkably straightforward. Questions of exactly what happened when (if at all) are for another time.

> Set yourself the task of writing the Old Testament story in under 700 words. Ensure that you include everything you consider to be an essential element of this outline (main characters, key events), and keep it succinct and to the point. Now learn it. Elaborate on it in different ways depending on real or imagined audiences to whom you might tell it. If you struggle with this, find other Christians to help and work on it together—then produce your own version(s). In a small group you might undertake in twos or threes the task of retelling the story in suitable ways for different audiences. You may be surprised at what other people see as the key elements in the Old Testament story; ask them why.

There is good precedent for this kind of thing. In Deut 6.20 we read, 'When your children ask you in time to come, "What is the meaning of the decrees and the statutes and the ordinances that the LORD our God has commanded you?"…' the answer is not given in the form of a theological treatise or of a bulk-standard sermon, but of a story—Israel's story to that point. And, in case one thinks that this is 'just for the kids,' when we get to the end of Joshua (ch 24, to be exact) all the tribes of Israel are gathered as Joshua retells Israel's story—which, notably, evokes a response of commitment to the LORD. Something similar happens when the Israelites return to Jerusalem to rebuild the temple following the Babylonian exile. Ezra (in Nehemiah 9) retells the story to the those who had returned and again evokes a response of commitment.

The answer is not given in the form of a theological treatise or of a bulk-standard sermon, but of a story

But this is not limited to the Old Testament. In Acts 7, Stephen defends himself when questioned by the high priest precisely by retelling Israel's story—with a particular slant that enraged his listeners. The telling and retelling of Israel's story is part of our heritage. It helped give our Israelite, Jewish and Christian forebears their identity and helped form their character—and so it could be with us also.

Individual Stories

So much for the 'Big Picture.' There is also much to be gained from reading individual stories within the Old Testament, and responding to them *as stories*. It is important that they fit within the bigger picture, but there is a time for focusing on one story for a while and responding to it in its own right. Rather than immediately looking for the 'timeless truth,' or asking what this passage tells the reader about God, or pondering about how to 'apply' this text today, try to follow the development of the plot and allow the narrator to guide you and amuse, startle, shock or baffle you as you proceed.

You might respond to the different characters as you would in other short stories. Good stories—and the Bible contains many of them—raise questions in the reader's mind and generate some kind of response. I imagine you, as I do, sometimes find yourself challenged by a good story (or a good film or play, for that matter) even when you read the story (or watched the film or play) primarily for its entertainment value. Good literature (and drama) works like that. It is a pleasure to read—or may even be agonising to read because of the responses it evokes, but gives a certain sense of satisfaction nonetheless. But at some level it also provokes deep thought and re-evaluation of some aspect of life.

Sometimes if we stop 'looking' for the message of a biblical story we find that it speaks in powerful and unexpected ways

It is my firm belief that biblical literature does this too. Sometimes if we stop 'looking' for the message of a biblical story, and immerse ourselves in it as literature we find that it speaks in powerful and unexpected ways. My guess is that much of the Old Testament was actually intended to function in this way, just as it seems Jesus' parables were. People listened to (and later read) the stories and enjoyed hearing them, but were often provoked to some response—awe, renewed commitment, change of lifestyle and perhaps, at times, rage at people within the story or even at God, or at the storyteller. Over time these stories played an important part in developing people's thinking and action, even when they were unaware of it.

Stories *do* have a major impact on how we think and act, and surely Christians should be allowing biblical stories to form their thinking and acting rather than the many other stories (or 'narratives') with which we are bombarded day by day. Read and enjoy the biblical stories; immerse yourself in them and allow them to shape your life—even when you are unaware that this is happening.

On your own, read a complete biblical story through and enjoy it as a story. Jonah might be a good one to start with, or perhaps Ruth. Then try to retell the story briefly. Note what has struck you as the key elements of the story, and what point(s) you are trying to convey in your retelling. It is good simply to read and enjoy stories, but you might like also to think about how the characters in the story are portrayed (including God), and how the plot (or storyline) develops. What seems to be the main point(s)? How is this point conveyed? What is the climax of the story?

A similar exercise can be undertaken in a small group. If everyone is prepared to read through a short story beforehand without trying to 'theologise' about it, but simply enjoying the story, it is fascinating to discover the very different ways people respond. Examining such things as characterisation, plot, point of view and timescale are also fruitful things to do in a group. Straight retelling of a story demonstrates what has struck people most deeply, and retelling the story in a different context (what might be an equivalent for the Jonah story today?) involves applying the story to contemporary Christian life.

You can find some examples of re-tellings of the biblical story on the Grove web site www.grovebooks.co.uk under Online Resources for this booklet. If you would like to send your own in, email it to office@grovebooks.co.uk and it can be added to the examples.

Philip Jenson

Writing a Psalm

3

Most Bible study methods focus on a specific passage and encourage readers to understand and apply what they have read.

An alternative approach is to teach a particular skill of reading a certain kind of text that can be then applied to similar ones. The following method not only does this, but also encourages a personal and creative response to a central biblical genre, the psalm. It is more of a workshop than a traditional Bible study. The final task of the study is to write a psalm, but this first requires an introduction to how the biblical writers composed a line of poetry and how they then built up the lines into a whole psalm with a particular mood and theme. The description below introduces various technical terms, but these are not necessary. As with most things, we learn best through example and imitation.

Parallelism

A line of biblical poetry usually consists of two parallel phrases (A, B) of about the same length. After the end of the first line there is a slight pause (/), at the end of the second a fuller pause (//). A typical line looks like this:

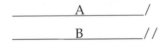

A very common form of parallelism is when A=B (*synonymous* parallelism). The two phrases present the same kind of thought. Often the elements of each phrase correspond.

He who sits in the heavens	laughs;
the Lord	has them in derision. (Ps 2.4)
Why do the nations	conspire,
and the peoples	plot in vain? (Ps 2.1)

In the second example an introductory word stands outside the strict parallelism. This often happens at the beginning of a section of a psalm (see Ps 1.1, 6.1).

Try completing the 'B' parallel to the following 'A' phrases. You can check what you have written against the original, but there is no 'correct' answer:

I will bless the LORD at all times...(Ps 34.1)
The nations have sunk in the pit that they have made...(Ps 9.15)

Another possible form of parallelism is when the meaning of the second phrase is the converse of that of the first (A≠B, *antithetic* parallelism).

O put an end to	the evil of the wicked
but establish	the righteous (Ps 7.9, adapted from NRSV)

for the LORD	watches over	the way of the righteous,
but	the way of the wicked	will perish. (Ps 1.6)

The last example shows a special technique that often occurs. The order of corresponding elements is reversed: 'watches over' is opposite to 'will perish,' and 'the way of the righteous' to 'the way of the wicked.' This is called *chiasmus*, and is a very fitting way to emphasize the ultimate reversal of the fates of the righteous and the wicked at the conclusion of the psalm. Other examples may be found in 1.2, 2.10.

Do the same for these examples:

For you deliver a humble people... (Ps 18.27)
Some take pride in chariots, and some in horses... (Ps 20.7)

There are many other kinds of parallelism, and various ways in which the two parts of a line can be related to one another, but these are sufficient for the purposes of this study.

Structure

A psalm is made up of verses that are each made up of two or three lines. Several of these verses then make up the entire poem, although longer psalms can also have larger divisions. Unfortunately the numbering of verses adopted by most translations (which are not part of the text but are a much later addition) do not always correspond to the psalm's own verse structure, but the principle is clear enough. Psalm 114 is a particularly clear example:

Verse numbers 1-2	2 lines	Verse 1	The Exodus people
Verse numbers 3-4	2 lines	Verse 2	Nature's witness
Verse numbers 5-6	2 lines	Verse 3	Nature's challenge
Verse numbers 7-8	2 lines	Verse 4	The Exodus God

Most of the psalms can be classified as either praise or lament. These are built up of the same kinds of units, although the way they are shaped and put together makes each psalm a unique creation. Because laments are more varied and complex, the task for this introductory Bible study will be to write a psalm of praise. The basic method can easily be extended for the writing of a psalm of lament.

A psalm of praise typically **begins** with a summons to the people to praise the Lord. For example (see also 111.1; 118.1-4):

> Praise the LORD!
> Praise, O servants of the LORD;
> praise the name of the LORD. (Ps 113.1)

The **main body** of a praise psalm consists of a number of reasons why the Lord should be praised, often indicated by a 'for.' These can be classified into two main areas. The first describes how God has acted on behalf of his people to save and establish them. This is sometimes called *declarative* praise, because Israel declares God's gracious deeds in history:

> He struck down many nations
> and killed mighty kings (Ps 135.10)

The second reason for praise is that God is the gracious creator and sustainer of the world. He has a constant character that is always evident and is the foundation for the way the world is. This is sometimes called *descriptive* praise:

> For the LORD, the Most High, is awesome,
> a great king over all the earth. (Ps 47.2)

A special kind of descriptive praise uses 'who' and the present tense (the *hymnic participle*):

> who forgives all your iniquity,
> who heals all your diseases (Ps 103.3)

> who by understanding makes the heavens,
> for his steadfast love endures forever
> (Ps 136.5; adapted from NRSV)

> who strikes Egypt through their firstborn,
> for his steadfast love endures forever
> (Ps 136.10; adapted from NRSV)

The NRSV translates the last two examples in the past tense, but this is a change from the Hebrew and reduces the impact of the lines for appreciating

God's character in the present. The lines are describing the abiding character of the God whom Israel knows as creator and saviour.

> Write two lines describing more of God's creative character using the hymnic participle ('who…').
>
> Write two lines declaring God's dramatic act of salvation in raising Jesus from the dead.

The **final part** of the psalm often includes a renewed summons to praise, similar in form to the opening summons (as in Ps 97.12). Sometimes the beginning and the end are exactly the same, a technique known as *inclusio* (118.1,29; 136.1,26). A number of psalms have 'praise the Lord' (*hallelujah* in Hebrew) at the beginning and the end, and these are known as hallelujah psalms (113;146-150).

Using this in a Bible Study

In the first part of the study the leader should introduce the main elements of writing a praise psalm. Participants have a go at writing their own lines, which may then be shared with a neighbour or with the group. The leader should ensure that the majority of participants understand the basic principles, perhaps by giving more worked examples. The second part of the study is the writing of an entire psalm, perhaps in groups of four. Each person can be given a particular part of the psalm to write, or this can be done jointly (which takes more time!). It may be helpful to appoint someone who can coordinate the contributions and read the whole psalm at the end. The psalms can also be used in the closing time of prayer and praise. It is probably helpful to set a specific theme if the psalm is to be written in a group (for example, the praise of a God who restores and heals).

Writing a psalm is an opportunity not just to put into practice the principles that have been learnt, but also to explore the character of God now known through Jesus Christ and at work in the present life of the church. Many of the great hymnic paraphrases of the psalms are just such creative meditations on the God of the Psalms now known more fully through Jesus Christ. Writing a psalm is a valuable invitation for individuals to express their specific insights into God's character and works. In a simplified form the same procedure might take the place of a sermon, especially in a smaller and more informal service. The various verses can be displayed on a screen with the help of a digital projector or an OHP screen. Good examples can be published in the parish magazine or on the church website. The ultimate purpose of the study is to deepen and enhance the way people will be able to read, understand, interpret and use the psalms in their own lives.

Margaret Killingray and Jo Bailey Wells

Flights of Fancy? Engaging the Imagination

4

because we are all
betrayers, taking
silver and eating
body and blood and asking
(guilty) is it I and hearing
him say yes
it would be simple for us all
to rush out
and hang ourselves

but if we find grace
to cry and wait
after the voice of morning
has crowed in our ears
clearly enough
to break our hearts
he will be there
to ask each again
do you love me

This poem, *Judas, Peter*, by Luci Shaw, combines several gospel events in a way that creates impact and draws insights out of already familiar stories. It has an impact on readers and hearers that may seldom be found in the ordinary processes of reading and hearing Scripture. It has brought deeper theological understanding of human guilt and of repentance, grace and forgiveness, where it has been used in Good Friday services. It illustrates the power of the creative imagination to reinforce scriptural teaching in ways that our run-of-the-mill, rational, orderly patterns of Bible reading may not always do.

Using the imagination requires discipline. I am not advocating a position in which 'anything goes'. Rather I believe the imagination needs training, just as other aspects of the mind need training—and that using the imagination is fufilling the command to love God with

Using the imagination requires discipline

our minds. As in the art of drawing, where there is discipline required in looking at a bowl of fruit, to see well and then portray it well on paper, so I am advocating a form of looking at a text in order to understand it and inhabit it. This requires some 'space' in a Bible study to allow such a process to happen and the trust not to interfere when it does. Bear in mind that for adults and for anyone with a very fixed view of Scripture, this sometimes involves an uncomfortable level of playfulness and risk!

But for those who teach and preach, and those who practise regular personal times of Bible reading, I would like to encourage the greater use of imaginative creativity in a number of ways and for a number of reasons.

Temperaments and systems

There is evidence that fewer Christians read the Bible frequently and regularly. Time pressure is a common factor cited in responses to surveys. For some, however, their difficulties arise because they assume that they should read the text in a certain way, sometimes having heard it expounded, passage-by-passage, in a particular format. The system of exposition they hear and the notes they use may well be driven by a particular theology of Scripture, which may imply disapproval of inductive methods and the use of the imagination. Yet preferred learning styles vary from individual to individual and personality differences mean that only a wide variety of approaches to teaching the text can meet the needs of congregations, in communal and individual learning. For some the slog involved in following some of the reading schemes that are available and the perceived pressure to be orthodox and systematic are too much.

The Bible itself by its very nature and variety needs different methods of approach

The Bible itself by its very nature and variety invites different methods of approach to the teaching and learning of the text. Only by using different and sometimes imaginative approaches can the whole of life in every aspect become involved with a living and life-changing text.

So, assuming that all those who are serious about making the Bible an integral part of all their thinking and doing will be spending regular times reading the text, then planning in some extra time to be actively creative and imaginative can be surprisingly rewarding, particularly for those who find routine and dated notes have a dulling affect.

Being creative

There are many ways in which we can incorporate the use of the imagination into our Bible reading. The most immediately available and simplest method is to imagine ourselves into the text by simply recreating the scene in our mind's eye, so that we are forced to read slowly and to take in every detail. This will be an obvious approach to narrative, but much of the wisdom literature with the rich use of metaphor also lends itself to mind's-eye reconstruction.

Much of the wisdom literature with the rich use of metaphor lends itself to mind's-eye reconstruction

The goal is so to enter into the story or scenario that one begins to identify with the people or events from the 'inside.' Nativity plays, at their best, function in this way. In playing the part of

Mary, my goddaughter recently found herself conscious of the weight of the baby in her arms and commenting on the burden of responsibility, holding such an important child. She identified with Mary as shy and confused by all those who come to visit, and embarrassed not to have clean clothes in which to put the baby. And my goddaughter tells me how cold it must have been for Mary, not only to be in a stable but after the exhaustion of giving birth. She wants to ask Joseph for help, and to trust God for the way forward…

I once introduced the story of 'doubting Thomas' (John 20) to some 10-year-olds by pretending that I had just been with David Beckham, and if they had only arrived for the school assembly a little earlier then they could have met him too! They knew I was joking, but I then asked how they would have felt had this really happened. Quick as a flash, one answered: 'Angry!' Ever since then I have called the disciple 'angry Thomas' and been keenly aware of the link between anger and unbelief.

The results of imaginative engagement cannot usually be predicted, but the outcome will enable those involved better to inhabit the biblical story—to see it from the inside—and so to place themselves before God.

An Ignatian Approach

The 'exercises' of Ignatius of Loyola were originally intended to encourage individuals to reflect on their own lives relative to the life of Christ. But the principles by which Ignatius outlines the exercises have proved valuable in other contexts, as a way of going beyond a purely intellectual reading of Scripture in search of more intuitive insights. The suggestions below may be used individually or within a group.

Read the passage slowly, allowing feeling to be expressed through the words. In some silence afterwards, seek to apply your imagination so as to recreate the scene. In a group context, this may be led by one person who shares their picture of the scene in colourful detail and leads others in the subsequent pattern of meditation. Put yourself in the position of one of the characters—continue this with others or even all the characters—and imagine what they are thinking and feeling and saying. Finally, place yourself within the scene and 'observe' what you feel like saying or doing; 'listen' to the response you receive from God or from other characters in the scene.

During this process, pay attention to anything that strikes a chord or produces a reaction in you—whether joy or fear or worry or confusion. If alone, pause here to explore the feeling, seeking to understand what is going on, whether positive or negative (Ignatius called these 'consolation' and 'desolation' respectively). In a group, this process might happen best during some shared silence, during which you might note the feelings raised so you can return to them—it is useful to have something on which to take notes. Afterwards, it can be valuable to talk about one's experience of the story—whether in the group context of sharing and prayer, or at some future opportunity with a friend, prayer partner or mentor.

A 'Godly Play' Approach

'Godly Play' is a system of religious education developed by Jerome Berryman, designed for children following a Montessori-style method. But the principles work equally well for adult readers of the Bible.

It involves re-telling a Bible story using some simple materials, such as a brown cloth to represent a desert scene, a strip of blue felt for a river and some wooden figures representing people. A study group might gather around this scene, set on a coffee table, as one person recounts the story following the biblical text closely. This is best done from memory, rather than with the text, so that all concerned can focus on the visual scene.

After the re-telling, the leader ends with some simple open invitations which begin with the words, 'I wonder…'. It is vital to this methodology that such 'wonderings' are not directly questions; rather, they are invitations to wonder together. There are no 'right' answers and no 'wrong' answers, merely thoughts to be shared. The idea is to give people permission to say anything—and often the first thing that comes to mind is the most valuable. This leads to a shared time of 'wondering', which may lead in an unforeseen direction as people respond to each other's offerings.

It is useful for the leader to remember four key 'wonderings' which can follow any story:

- I wonder what part of this story you liked the best?
- I wonder what part of this story is the most important?
- I wonder what part of this story is really about you?
- I wonder what part of this story you could have managed without and still had all the story you needed?

The leader should leave plenty of space for reflection and response. He or she might be wise to have some further lines of wondering specific to the particular story up his or her sleeve. These should be worded carefully so as to open up various possible responses, rather than seek a single 'right' response. So for example, with the story of the baptism of Christ (Luke 3):

- I wonder what kinds of people were in the crowd listening to John preach?
- I wonder how it felt for John to see Jesus approaching?
- I wonder how people responded to the dove?

The leader's role is to open up the wondering and then to enjoy it along with the rest of the group, rather than respond to each offering. It is important that the leader does not seek to comment on anything that is offered—like a teacher—but to create a safe environment and then to trust the process.

Dramatic Reading and Rendition

This is perhaps a more conventional technique: to assign to different members of a group a role or part to take on, and to read or act the Bible story within the group. One easy way to do this is by means of *The Dramatised Bible* (GNB/NIV) which divides the text into relevant voices. If the group is larger than the number of roles, then two or more people might share one role by discussing the character and portrayal together before and afterwards.

This method allows individuals to engage carefully with the story from the angle of one particular player. It does this directly, verbally and publicly and would suit a lively, talkative group in contrast to the Ignatian approach which is more meditative, intuitive and 'interior.'

This method allows individuals to engage carefully with the story from the angle of one particular player

In discussion afterwards I would encourage, first of all, that group members participate 'in role,' that is, that they maintain their casting and debate the incident as they found it from that 'inside' perspective. It can then become a useful exercise in itself to step out of that role, and in the de-briefing to reflect on what that character might have to say to the 'real' you and vice versa.

A further stage might be to re-play the story once more, with group members each taking on a different role—and relating how differently the story looks from a different perspective.

There are a number of ways in which the public reading of the Bible in church services can be dramatised or made memorable, thus enabling the involvement of those listening. These can also be adapted for small group use; for further details see Grove Worship booklet W 177 *How to Read the Bible in Church*.

Other Ideas

The use of **creative writing** can also be enormously helpful. This can take the form of extracting some topic, or person, from the text and using imaginative reconstruction to flesh out the sometimes cryptic and sparse details we are given.

* Imagine you are a Christian in prison as a result of Paul's persecution of the church. You hear of his conversion. What are your feelings, your emotions? How might you react on meeting him?
* Reflect on the nature and dimensions of a perfect city, pulling together all the material on Jerusalem, in the Psalms, Revelation, and the gospels.
* Reflect on one of the metaphors used to describe God's rescuing or protective power. You might use the internet to collect images of towers, shields, parenting, chickens sheltering their young, and so on.

The **linking of current situations**, personal as well as national and international, to Bible passages can also be valuable. As the Prayer Book marriage service links Cana with getting married, so events of great importance may gain significance by some textual link. For example, the story of Jonathan and his relationships with David and his father, Saul, can be used to reflect on and pray for those we know with divided loyalties and family tensions. This kind of approach can be very helpful in group Bible study, where current examples, worldwide, of famine, war, celebration, natural disaster can be linked to similar examples in the text, giving insights into the text and encouraging Bible linked prayer for world situations.

Why not **keep a journal**, even in scrapbook form, where you can allow yourself to record even the most divergent creative thinking.

Finding **themes in film, music and literature** can also be effective. Watching the film *Master and Commander* reminded me of the importance of an understanding of the powerful imagery of sea, waves and storms in the Bible. There is a wealth of creative material that can help our understanding, learning and retention of biblical teaching. In music, Mendelssohn's *Elijah* conjures up the prophet's praying to God on Carmel. In art, Rembrandt's *The Return of the Prodigal* has been used to great effect as providing a way into Jesus' parable in Luke 15. Photographs, not just beautiful 'coffee table book' ones, but journalist's photographs, and our own, can be used to illuminate biblical themes. Some of the scenes from Dorothy L Sayers' *The Man Born to be King*, although rather dated now, can add striking dimensions to the gospel story.

Possibilities and Limitations

Imaginative interpretation works best with the narrative parts of Scripture, such as the gospels and Acts in the New Testament, and the narrative parts of Genesis, Exodus and Samuel-Kings in the Old Testament. It is harder—though perhaps not impossible!—to use these techniques with more didactic or legal genres.

One important advantage of imaginative approaches over traditional Bible study methods is that it is inclusive in groups of varied age range. In fact, children are often better able to engage the imagination than adults, being less constrained by convention. This makes for an exciting group process whereby the adults have much to gain from the contribution of younger members—genuinely an all-age experience!

This makes for an exciting group process whereby the adults have much to gain from the contribution of younger members

Time is one of the most mentioned factors in surveys of Bible reading. Finding time to read at all, being realistic about time, is the greatest challenge for many, let alone building in more time-consuming practices, however worthwhile.

Imaginative and creative reading of the Bible on one's own can be a little disconcerting, perhaps even embarrassing, but can take off when built in to group study.

We do need to keep an eye on where creativity is taking us

There does need to be firm grounding in what the text actually says. It is possible to imagine oneself right out of the context and meaning of the passage. In an exercise recreating the healing of the boy with fits, after the Transfiguration, we found that a great deal depended on whether the boy had epilepsy, as in the GNB, had been 'moonstruck' by the moon 'god', or was possessed by a demon. We do need to keep an eye on where creativity is taking us.

We need also to be aware of the possibility of God speaking out of a passage in words beyond the Word. Sometimes, especially if we are allowing time for our imagination to work us through a passage, we can sense a message that is not integral to the text. This is one area where meditation, prayer and discussion in groups can be helpful as we test each other's insights.

5

Images at the Service of Bible Reading

We live in a world increasingly dominated and fascinated by imagery in magazines, books, TV and film.

Learning to read cultural values in images of the world around is essential for Christian communication that connects today. Here we will narrow the focus to how images based on Scripture can help or hinder us in Bible reading. Not all biblical texts are equally susceptible to artistic treatment. Narrative and poetic imagery are more commonly turned into images than law, letters or prophetic writings. Old Testament stories are favourites. The gospel stories have been a central focus of inspiration for the artistic imagination. Paintings, like Holman Hunt's famous *Light of the World,* are unusual in depicting combinations of texts and focussing on theological ideas.

Opening Up and Closing Down

Seeing the text expressed in (other people's) images has advantages. It reminds us explicitly of what we regularly do with texts quite instinctively—turn them into a mental imagery. Encountering someone else's image of a text challenges our imagination to think anew about our own presuppositions and assumptions about the text. When it was first shown Caravaggio's *The Road to Emmaus* (see www.kfki.hu/~arthp/html/c/caravagg/06/35emmau.html) raised a storm of protest from the Church. Christ was beardless, plump and associated with ordinary, poor people. Four hundred years on, the insights that Jesus associated with the lowly and was hard to recognize in his resurrection are hard to fault from the gospels. Caravaggio's artistic realism challenged the accepted religious imagination to new theological insights. In Mel Gibson's film *The Passion of the Christ,* the dreadful scenes of Christ's scourging and crucifixion act to bridge the cultural gap that has been opened up by our 2,000-year distance from the realities of crucifixion. Public taste and centuries of Christian theology might dull the dread of the word 'cross' if we do not allow our imaginations to be renewed. Images can open up our imaginative world.

Unfortunately images can also do the opposite. They can close down our imaginative world by supplanting the Word with a striking but fixed image. Holman Hunt's *The Light of the World* (www.artchive.com/artchive/H/hunt/

hunt_light_of_world.jpg.html) shows Jesus carrying a lamp, in a dark wood, knocking on the handle-less door of a overgrown cottage. Stock image of countless evangelistic sermons, it depicts Revelation 3.20: 'Behold I stand at the door and knock,' a verse actually directed at half-hearted Christians, not unbelievers. However, Hunt also used the rich 'light' imagery of John's Gospel (3.19–21; 5.35; 8.12; 9.10; 12.36, 36, 46). This is the language of decision for every human: Will you come from the darkness out into the light of Christ, or will you avoid the light and prefer darkness? Hunt's picture actually distorts our interpretation of Revelation 3.20 by becoming the spectacles through which we view the text. Fortunately the Fourth Gospel's imagery, though different, is just to the point. I have often wondered at the opportunity missed in pictures of the OT Samson stories (Judges 13–16) which show him to be tall and muscular, as if he was some ancient version of Arnold Schwarzenegger. A puny Samson would make the point of the story: power is from God not our own innate resources.

Text and Image

One way to ensure that an image does not close down our imaginative horizons is simply to compare the text with the image based on it. Here is a British newspaper cartoon from 1997. It is worth stopping now and taking a few minutes to look at the image before reading the explanation. Think about these questions: What biblical text is this based on?

Who are the four riders? What do they represent? Where are they riding? What might the message of the cartoon be?

This image accompanied an article about the European Union. It was based loosely on Revelation 6.1–8, the fours riders on coloured horses summoned to the first four judgements of God upon the earth. As the Lamb breaks each of the seals the figures of conquest (6.1–2), war (6.3–4), famine (6.5–6) and death (6.7–8) are unleashed. Revelation's imagery expresses the judgement of God but also says that it begins as limited judgement (see 6.6b, 8b). Later it will intensify as the series of judgements (seals, trumpets, bowls) unfolds. In other words it acts as a warning that not everything is under human control but that God reigns and that he will bring his judgement on the earth.

Our contemporary artist (Dave Brown) imagines four potential horrors stalking modern Europe—private armies/international terrorism, industrial pollution, street violence and nuclear meltdown. Each of these threats to democracy and political stability is not local or national but trans-national and beyond the scope of national governments acting alone. If the EU cannot deal with problems like these, then it is not doing its job and all hope is lost. These contemporary riders are symbols of the limitations of human political power and they shake our confidence in human control—which is precisely the point of the riders in Revelation 6. But Revelation also proposes an alternative. Disaster is not just a random series of events; the world is under the rule of God and for rejecting this it is also under the judgement of God. It is he who controls human history and the destiny of nations—which takes us back to the cartoon image. How good a representation of today's sources of conquest, war, famine and death do you think the cartoon images are? And what might people around us think is the alternative to human control over the events of human history? Do they think that anyone is in charge?

Images like this one are not simple representations of the biblical text. They take up the biblical imagery and relate it to today's world. They do so in ways that open up the horizons of our imagination. They face us with important interpretative and missiological questions: How does this text speak today in relevant language that the person in the street can understand?

Another way of preventing images from closing down rather than opening up our horizons is to compare images of the same biblical text. Compare the cartoon on p 21 with William Blake's dream-like watercolour based on Revelation. You can find it at www.artmagick.com/paintings/painting4205.aspx or look under Online Resources at www.grovebooks.co.uk. Spend some time looking at the picture. One warning and one hint. The *warning* is that Blake has indulged in the common error of identifying the Rider of Revelation 6.1–2 with the Rider of Revelation 19.11ff. What are the problems of identifying these two Riders with one another? The *hint* is that Blake's painting is a masterpiece of condensation and conflation. How many horses can you see?

It is great simply to appreciate art for its imagination or beauty, but it is also important to read it theologically if we are to read culture alongside the Bible. Used discerningly, images can open up our imaginative horizons to the biblical text. Used uncritically, they can subvert the Word by replacing the text with a fixed but imagined version of it. Freeing the imagination should take us closer to the biblical text not further from it—as my title implies, images need to serve our reading of the Bible, not control it.

Michael B Thompson

Charting Scripture

6

Another way to deepen and refresh Bible study is by making your own charts.

The process of making a chart requires you to think about *relationships* between words, clauses, sentences and paragraphs in the text. It is in those relationships that you more clearly see the logic and structure of smaller or larger units in the Bible. Thinking through those relationships helps you not only to understand but also to remember the text, so that it becomes a part of you.

Charts are not an end in themselves (unless the goal is to create material to teach to others); the value of the exercise lies in the *process* of becoming more familiar with the passage and letting it soak into you, rather than in the *result* produced on paper. So the first point to keep in mind when beginning to 'chart' the Bible is that it is perfectly all right to make a mess! Recording your observations and insights in an exercise of listening to God is far more important than producing a neat and orderly chart.

Marking up the Text

There are *many* different kinds of charts; this chapter will briefly introduce three. The simplest is to turn the text itself into a chart, by marking up a paragraph or two of Scripture that has been photocopied, scanned or printed out using Bible software. Writing over a copy of the text can give you the freedom to scribble ideas and observations right where you see them without spoiling your bound Bible.

Every time I prepare to preach or teach a passage of scripture, I use computer software to print out the text (in as large a typeface as possible, leaving room in the margins and between lines of text) on a single sheet of paper. This gives me the space to 'dig in' and to see the individual bits and emphases in clauses (a group of words, including at least a subject and verb that comprise a partial or whole unit of thought and expression) sentences and paragraphs. It also helps me to spot interpretative difficulties that I will need to spend more time on later.

I begin by using coloured pens or pencils to circle or underline key words. Examples of such words include terms that are repeated in the text, and particularly the main points made at the beginning and end of paragraphs. I keep in mind the reporter's questions ('Who?', 'What?', 'When?', 'Where?', 'Why?', 'How?', plus 'So What?'). I mark the linking words such as 'because,' 'therefore,' 'if,' 'when' that say something about the logical, geographical or temporal structure of the passage.

I also find it useful to draw and label arrows to link different parts of the text that are related in some way. Here are some examples of relationships to look for, with suggested passages in which you can find them. They are derived in part from Robert Traina's *Methodical Bible Study* (Zondervan, 2002):

Purpose (John 20.30–31)

Result (movement from cause to effect; Romans 1.18–30)

Example (Hebrews 11)

Repetition (use of the *same* word or phrase repeatedly; 1 Cor 13)

Question (Rom 6)

Explanation (Mark 4)

Interchange (alternating bits to strengthen contrasts or comparisons, such as the alternation between Hannah and her son Samuel with Eli and his sons in 1 Sam 1–4)

Summarization (Rom 1.16–17)

Contrast (Matt 5.17–48; Galatians 5)

Comparison (Hebrews 5.1–10; Romans 5.12–21)

Continuity (repeated use of *similar* words or phrases, such as the series of parables in Luke 15)

Climax (Exodus 40.34–35)

These relationships indicate what the biblical author is doing as he tells his story or moves from one idea to another.

The use of colour in this kind of charting makes it easier to keep different insights and observations separate. The more you mark up your text, the more complicated it becomes, and the more difficult it is to see the individual bits. You may find that you need to print out another base copy to give you the space to record your final impressions as you come to the end of your study.

Horizontal Layouts

One way of charting that is particularly useful for gaining an overview of larger blocks of text is the horizontal layout (see the chart of Mark 11:27–12.44 on the following page). This involves drawing a line down most of the length of a piece of paper, and using the line as a base upon which you plot the paragraphs (or chapters if you are studying a longer text). Turn the page sideways and using a ruler, draw enough short parallel lines coming up from the base to enclose the number of segments (paragraphs, sections, or chapters) you plan to study. So the base of my example chart originally looked something like this:

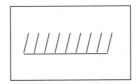

As you read through the text, give a short title to each segment that represents your best effort to summarize its main point (or topic), writing the title into the spaces created by your parallel lines. Do not give in to the temptation to copy section titles out of your Bible (if it has them)—make up your own! In my example, I gave the title 'question of authority' to the first segment in the passage I was studying, then 'wicked tenants' to the second segment and so on.

Once you have titled your segments, begin to look at the relationships between them. Using different colours (if possible) note these relationships down on your chart, with arrows or brief explanations if you need them. In my passage, the fact that Jesus' statement in Mark 12.34 put an end to the series of questions people asked him makes it function as a sort of mini-climax, and the sincerity of the widow in 12.41ff forms a sharp contrast with the hypocrisy of the scribes in the preceding paragraph.

When you have become very familiar with the text, try to see if any segments belong together in a larger thematic group. If they do, lengthen the appropriate dividing lines to make the groupings clear. In my example, I lengthened the lines dividing Mark 12.12 and 12.13 and between 12.34 and 12.35, because the more I studied the text, the more it seemed to me that major changes happened in those places.

If you find it helpful, you can use the space below the baseline to record observations about time, geography, characters, key words or themes. Once again, the use of colour can be very helpful. For long books such as the gospels, I have taped two pieces of paper end-to-end in order to create enough segments to have one for each chapter. The important thing is to feel free to use whatever method that helps you to mine the text for its precious ore.

Mark 11:27-12:44
Jesus Teaches in the Temple

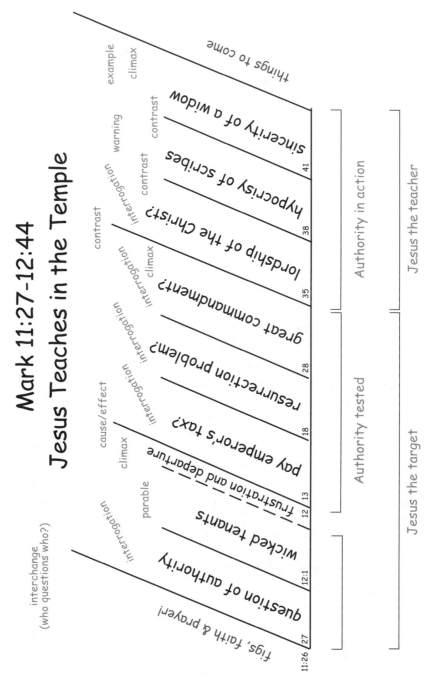

interchange
(who questions who?)

interrogation

figs, faith & prayer!

11:26 27

question of authority

parable

wicked tenants

12:1

frustration and departure

12 13

pay emperor's tax?

climax

cause/effect

18

resurrection problem?

interrogation

28

great commandment?

interrogation

35

lordship of the Christ?

climax

interrogation

contrast

38

hypocrisy of scribes

interrogation

contrast

41

sincerity of a widow

warning

contrast

example
climax

things to come

contrast

Authority in action

Authority tested

Jesus the teacher

Jesus the target

Grammatical Layouts

Another kind of chart is the grammatical layout. This method is particularly useful with individual verses or with a paragraph of text. The aim is to reflect the structure of the text in the way you arrange all of the words of the passage, either by hand or with a word processor. For example, Acts 1.8 can be expressed this way:

But
> you will receive power
>> when the Holy Spirit has come upon you;

and
> you will be my witnesses
>> in Jerusalem,
>> in all Judea and Samaria,
> and
>> to the ends of the earth.

Grammatically, the clauses 'you will receive power' and 'you will be my witnesses' are parallel and form the heart of this verse. Laying out the text in grammatical form helps you to see the emphases in a text, as well as enabling you to spot important subpoints. It also gives you space to write your observations about what you find there.

Do not be put off by the assumption that your English grammar has to be good to use this method. You are perfectly able to spot the structure of a text without knowing the technical terms for its constituent bits. The value of this method, like those of the other methods in this chapter, lies in sharpening the questions you fire at the text. The more questions you ask, the more you shall receive!

7 Further Resources

Enjoying the Story

Lesslie Newbigin, *A Walk Through the Bible* (Triangle, 1999). A short book, the write-up of two powerful talks Newbigin gave in London summarising the story of the Bible.

Richard Bauckham, Grove Biblical booklet B 2 *Is the Bible Male?* Some fascinating insights into Ruth as women's literature.

Philip Jenson, Grove Biblical booklet B 14 *Reading Jonah*. Engaging study highlighting Jonah's power as a story.

Writing a Psalm

John Goldingay, Grove Spirituality booklet S 44 *Praying the Psalms*, now available as a chapter in Ian Paul (ed) *Building Your Spiritual Life* (Zondervan, 2003).

Engaging the Imagination

The Spiritual Exercises of St Ignatius (New York: Doubleday, 1989).

John Goldingay, Grove Biblical booklet B 24 *An Ignatian Approach to Reading the Old Testament*.

M Perry (ed), *The Dramatised Bible* (London: Marshall Pickering 1989).

S M Stewart and J W Berryman, *Young Children and Worship* (Louisville, KY: Westminster John Knox, 1989)

A daily Ignatian meditation, 'Sacred Space', is available online thanks to the Irish Jesuits http://www.jesuit.ie/prayer/

Charting Scripture

Oletta Wald, *The New Joy of Discovery in Bible Study* (Augsburg Fortress Publishers, 2002). A new edition of a classic that first appeared in 1959 that will take individuals and groups deep into inductive Bible study.

Robert Traina, *Methodical Bible Study* (Zondervan, 2002). First published in 1952 and even more thorough than Wald, though a little dated in its references.